T0153456

THE LITTLE BOOK OF
WAR POETS

Published in 2023 by OH!
An Imprint of Welbeck Non-Fiction Limited,
part of Welbeck Publishing Group.
Offices in London – 20 Mortimer Street, London W1T 3JW
and Sydney – Level 17, 207 Kent St, Sydney NSW 2000 Australia
www.welbeckpublishing.com

ISBN 978-1-80069-551-1

Written and compiled by: Grace Beattie
Editorial: Matt Thomlinson
Project manager: Russell Porter
Design: Ravina Patel
Production: Jess Brisley
A CIP catalogue record for this book is available from the British Library

Printed in China

10 9 8 7 6 5 4 3 2 1

THE LITTLE BOOK OF

WAR POETS

ANTHEMS FOR DOOMED YOUTH

CONTENTS

INTRODUCTION

War has been a defining feature of the human experience since ancient times. From the earliest battles between warring tribes to the huge mechanized conflicts of the modern age, poets have felt compelled to respond: to celebrate heroism and victories, to mourn and honour the fallen, and to capture the brutality and the terrible human toll.

When war poetry is mentioned today, it immediately recalls the great soldier poets of the First World War. We think of the poignant idealism expressed in poems such as Rupert Brooke's "The Soldier", written in the first year of the war: "If I should die, think only this of me / That there's some corner of a foreign field / That is for ever England"; and of the visceral descriptions of mud, shells and slaughter found in poems such as Wilfred Owen's "The Sentry": "We dredged him up, for killed, until he whined / 'O Sir, my eyes – I'm blind – I'm blind, I'm blind!'"

First World War poetry is often considered a genre in

itself because of the unique characteristics and themes that define it. Many of the poets who wrote during this time were themselves soldiers, giving their work a sense of raw authenticity. Before this conflict, war poetry was largely intended to celebrate courage and victories, and to commemorate the fallen. Since 1918, it has become predominantly anti-war – a recognition of how war, despite being a human phenomenon, strips away our humanity.

This little book focuses mainly on the First World War poets, but also looks at war poetry across the ages. From the epic poems of ancient Greece to the haunting elegies of medieval Europe, and from the martial odes of the Roman Empire to the bitter anti-war poems of the modern day, it brims with powerful and poignant quotes. Excerpts are often accompanied by fascinating information about the poets, providing a unique insight into the ways in which war has shaped the human experience.

CHAPTER

1

THE NOBLE WARRIOR

It was the First World War Poets who established war poetry as a genre of its own, but war poems have a long and varied history.

Unlike modern anti-war poems, the earliest war songs — such as Homer's *The Iliad* — were generally celebrations of battle, exploring themes of heroism, bravery and sacrifice. Medieval poetry often idealized the warrior as a noble figure, while the Romantic poets celebrated both the beauty and the horror of battle.

Enheduanna (23rd century BCE) was a priestess in the kingdom of ancient Sumeria.

She is often described as the world's first author, and her poem "Lament to the Spirit of War" is believed to be the very first war poem.

> **"**
> You hack down everything you
>   see, War God!
> Rising on fearsome wings
> you rush to destroy the land:
> raging like thunderstorms,
> howling like hurricanes,
> screaming like tempests…**"**

ENHEDUANNA
"Lament to the Spirit of War", 23rd century BCE

The ancient Greek poet Homer
(c. 750 BCE) composed *The Iliad*, a
timeless, epic poem that vividly evokes
the horror, loss and agony at the
heart of the Trojan War.

It is a classic work of literature
that explores themes of honour, pride
and glory, as well as the tragedy
of war.

"

The Wrath of Achilles is my theme, that fatal wrath which, in fulfillment of the will of Zeus, brought the Achaeans so much suffering and sent the gallant souls of many nobleman to Hades, leaving their bodies as carrion for the dogs and passing birds.

"

HOMER

The Iliad, 8th century BCE

During the First World War,
Patrick Shaw-Stewart (1888–1917),
an Oxford classics scholar, fought at
Gallipoli – just across the Hellespont
(or Dardanelles) from Troy.

In his only war poem, written just
before he arrived at Gallipoli, he
heavily references Homer's *The Iliad*.
Shaw-Stewart was killed in action
in France.

"

Was it so hard, Achilles,
So very hard to die?
Thou knowest, and I know not;
So much the happier am I.

I will go back this morning
From Imbros o'er the sea.
Stand in the trench, Achilles,
Flame-capped, and shout for me.

"

PATRICK SHAW STEWART

From "Achilles in the Trench", 1915

"

Go tell the Spartans,
you who read:
We took their orders
and are dead.

"

SIMONIDES OF CEOS

Epitaph for the 300 Spartans who fought and died
at Thermopylae against the Persian invasion in 480 BCE

Nearly 1,500 years after Greek poet Simonides of Ceos wrote his epitaph for the dead of Thermopylae, Rudyard Kipling (1865–1936) penned one for the dead of the First World War.

"

If any question why we died,
Tell them, because our
    fathers lied.

"

RUDYARD KIPLING

"Common Form", from *Epitaphs of the War, 1914–18*

The epic poem *The Aeneid*, composed by the Roman poet Virgil between 29 and 19 BCE, centres around the Trojan War and its aftermath, with Aeneas leading his fellow Trojans on a perilous journey to establish a new home in Italy.

The poem explores themes such as the brutality of warfare, the psychological toll it takes on soldiers, and the role of fate in determining the outcome of battles.

"

Alike the victors and the
vanquished slew and fell.
Nor these, not those know what it
is to flee.
The gods above with pitying
eyes behold
The fruitless rage of both, and
grieve to see
Such woes for mortal men.

"

VIRGIL

From *The Aeneid*, Book 10

The renowned Chinese poet
Li Po (701–762 CE) of the Tang Dynasty
railed against the futility of war.

"Nefarious War", which criticizes the
generals who have "accomplished
nothing", could be a poem from the
First World War.

"

In the battlefield men grapple
each other and die;
The horses of the vanquished utter
lamentable cries to heaven…

So, men are scattered and
smeared over the desert grass,
And the generals have
accomplished nothing.

"

LI PO
From "Nefarious War", 750 CE

"

There was a crashing of shields.
Seafarers came forth enraged in
the fight;
The spear often went right
through the life-houses of the
fated…

They stood fast, warriors in the
warfare, warriors perishing,
warriors wearied by wounds.
The slain fell to the earth.

99

From an Old English poem describing
the Battle of Maldon between an Anglo-Saxon army and
invading Vikings, in 991 CE. The poet is unknown.

> **"**
> We few, we happy few, we band of brothers;
> For he to-day that sheds his blood with me
> Shall be my brother…
> **"**

WILLIAM SHAKESPEARE

From *Henry V*, Act IV, Scene III, 1599

"

I hate that drum's discordant sound,
Parading round, and round, and round:
To thoughtless youth it pleasure yields,
And lures from cities and from fields,
To sell their liberty for charms
Of tawdry lace, and glittering arms;
And when Ambition's voice commands,
To march, and fight, and fall,
    in foreign lands.

"

JOHN SCOTT

From "The Drum", 1782

"The Battle of Blenheim", an anti-war poem by English Romantic poet Robert Southey (1774–1843), imagines two small children finding a skull at the battle site.

Their grandfather tells them about burned homes and thousands of rotting corpses, but he cannot explain what the purpose of the war was – other than to say, "But things like that, you know, must be / After a famous victory".

"

'And everybody praised the Duke
Who this great fight did win.'
'But what good came of it at last?'
Quoth little Peterkin.
'Why, that I cannot tell,' said he,
'But 'twas a famous victory.'

"

ROBERT SOUTHEY

The Battle of Blenheim, 1796

"

Must we but weep o'er days
    more blest?
Must we but blush? – Our fathers bled.
Earth! render back from out thy
    breast
A remnant of our Spartan dead!
Of the three hundred grant but three,
To make a new Thermopylae!

"

LORD BYRON

From "The Isles of Greece", 1819

"

The Assyrian came down like the
wolf on the fold,
And his cohorts were gleaming in
purple and gold;
And the sheen of their spears was
like stars on the sea,
When the blue wave rolls nightly
on deep Galilee.

"

LORD BYRON

From "The Destruction of Sennacherib", telling the
biblical story of the failed Assyrian siege of Jerusalem, 1815

29

"The Charge of the Light Brigade",
by Alfred Lord Tennyson (1809–92),
famously celebrates an act of bravery
and sacrifice during the Crimean war.

Written six weeks after the
Battle of Balaklava (1854), Tennyson
argues that the willingness of the
British cavalry to sacrifice themselves
in the disastrous charge against heavily
defended Russian troops – without
calling their orders into question –
makes them heroes.

"

When can their glory fade?
O the wild charge they made!
All the world wondered.
Honour the charge they made!
Honour the Light Brigade,
Noble six hundred!

"

ALFRED LORD TENNYSON

"The Charge of the Light Brigade", 1854

American poet Ralph Waldo Emerson (1803–82) wrote "Concord Hymn" for an 1837 Independence Day celebration.

The poem celebrates the courage and sacrifice of the American patriots who fought at the Battle of Concord, at the beginning of the American Revolutionary War.

It has become an iconic symbol of American history and patriotism.

"

By the rude bridge that arched
  the flood,
Their flag to April's breeze
  unfurled,
Here once the embattled
  farmers stood
And fired the shot heard round
  the world.

"

RALPH WALDO EMERSON
"Concord Hymn", 1854

"

Mine eyes have seen the glory
of the coming of the Lord:
He is trampling out the vintage
where the grapes of wrath are
stored;
He hath loosed the fateful lightning
of His terrible swift sword:
His truth is marching on.

"

JULIA WARD HOWE

"The Battle Hymn of the Republic", 1862

> **Mother whose heart hung
> humble as a button
> On the bright splendid
> shroud of your son,
> Do not weep.
> War is kind.**

STEPHEN CRANE

From "War is Kind", 1899

CHAPTER

2

PRIDE AND PATRIOTISM

THROUGHOUT HISTORY, WAR POETS HAVE CELEBRATED THE BRAVERY OF SOLDIERS WILLING TO LAY DOWN THEIR LIVES FOR THEIR COUNTRY.

SUCH IDEALISM WAS MUCH IN EVIDENCE AT THE OUTBREAK OF THE FIRST WORLD WAR, BUT AS THE CASUALTIES MOUNTED, POETS SUCH AS SIEGFRIED SASSOON AND WILFRED OWEN – WHO HAD WITNESSED FIRST-HAND THE HORROR OF THE TRENCHES – ARGUED THAT SUCH BLIND PATRIOTISM OBSCURED THE SUFFERING OF THE SOLDIERS AND, IN OWEN'S WORDS, "THE PITY OF WAR".

"

Without a sign, his sword the
brave man draws,
and asks no omen, but his
country's cause.

"

HOMER

The Iliad, 8th century BCE

“

Let me not then die ingloriously
and without a struggle,
but let me first do some great
thing that shall be told among
men hereafter.

”

HOMER

Hector, as he realizes he is about to die at Achilles' hand,
The Iliad, 8th century BCE

"

To arms, to arms! my jolly grenadiers!
Hark how the drums do roll it along!…
Let not your courage fail you;
Be valiant, stout, and bold;
And it will soon avail you,
My loyal hearts of gold.
Huzzah, my valiant countrymen! –
    again I say huzzah!
'Tis nobly done, – the day's our own –
    huzzah, huzzah!

"

STEPHEN TILDEN

From "Fortduquesue Expedition", 1755

66

Then out spoke brave Horatius,
the Captain of the Gate:
To every man upon this earth,
death cometh soon or late;
And how can man die better
than facing fearful odds,
For the ashes of his fathers,
and the temples of his Gods.

99

THOMAS BABINGTON MACAULAY

From "Horatius", *Lays of Ancient Rome*, 1842

William Wordsworth's (1770–1850) masterpiece, *The Prelude*, captures the excitement and idealism that many felt in the early days of the French Revolution, before the violence and bloodshed of the Reign of Terror.

It illustrates the seductive power of war and the ways in which it can transform even the most mundane aspects of life into something thrilling and romantic.

66

Bliss was it in that dawn to
be alive,
But to be young was very
Heaven!

99

WILLIAM WORDSWORTH

The Prelude, Book XI, 1850

"

The river of death has brimmed
    his banks,
And England's far, and Honour
    a name,
But the voice of a schoolboy rallies
    the ranks,
'Play up! Play up! And play
    the game!'

"

HENRY NEWBOLT

From "Vitaï Lampada" ("They Pass on the Torch of Life"), 1892.
The engagement refers to the Battle of Abu Klea in Sudan,
in 1885.

"

To count the life of battle good,
And dear the land that gave
  you birth,
And dearer yet the brotherhood
That binds the brave of all
  the earth.

"

HENRY NEWBOLT

From "Clifton Chapel", 1908

The first months of the First World War saw the writing of many patriotic songs intended to boost morale and rally support for the Empire's cause.

However, as the casualty figures steadily mounted, songs that concentrated on an end to the fighting became increasingly popular. "Keep the Home Fires Burning" and "When Tommy Comes Marching Home" were typical.

"

Oh! we don't want to lose you
   but we think you ought to go,
For your King and your
Country both need you so…

"

PAUL RUBENS

From "Your King and Country Want You",
a popular recruiting song, 1914

"

Keep the home fires burning,
While your hearts are yearning.
Though your lads are far away
They dream of home.

"

IVOR NOVELLO

From "Keep the Home Fires Burning", 1915

"

Take me back to dear old Blighty!
Put me on the train for London
    town!
Take me over there,
Drop me anywhere,
Liverpool, Leeds, or Birmingham,
Well, I don't care!

"

**ARTHUR J MILLS, FRED GODFREY
AND BENNETT SCOTT**

From "Take Me Back to Dear Old Blighty", 1916

66

Upon the shores of Anzac
In many a nameless grave,
Australia's sons are sleeping,
Her heroes, true and brave.

99

LE HOMFRAY

From "Voice of Anzac", 1917

66

And though there's never a
grave to tell,
Nor a cross to mark his fall,
Thank God! we know that he
"batted well"
In the last great Game of all.

99

ROBERT SERVICE

From "The Fool", 1916

"The Soldier", by Rupert Brooke (1887–1915), was read aloud during the Easter Sunday service at St Paul's in London in 1915.

The poem, with its hopeful idealism and unabashed patriotism, caught the mood of the time.

"

If I should die,
  think only this of me:
That there's some corner of a
  foreign field
That is for ever England.

"

ROBERT BROOKE

From "The Soldier", 1915

Like many young men of his background, Rupert Brooke immediately volunteered for service in the war.

In 1915, while sailing to the Dardanelles for the Gallipoli campaign, he died from an infected mosquito bite, at the age of 27.

His death was keenly felt throughout his country, with Winston Churchill remarking, "He was all that one would wish England's noblest sons to be."

As the casualties continued to mount through 1916 and 1917, the patriotic sentiments expressed in Brooke's verse began to seem naive.

As poet John Lehmann wrote, "What soldier, who had experienced the meaningless horror and foulness of the Western Front stalemate in 1916 and 1917, could think of it as a place to greet 'as swimmers into cleanness leaping' or as a welcome relief 'from a world grown old and cold and weary'?"

"

Go, and may the God of battles
You in his good guidance keep:
And if he wisdom giveth
Unto his beloved sleep
I accept nothing asking,
    save little space to weep.

"

WN HODGSON

From "England to her Sons", 1914.
Hodgson was killed on the first day of the
Battle of the Somme, 1916.

"

From the thousand years of glory,
    from the grave of heroes gone,
Comes a voice on the breath of the
    storm, and a power to spur us on:
A man must now be a man,
    and every man be true,
From the grave that covers our glory
    shall cover each Briton too.

"

FREDERICK GEORGE SCOTT

From "Song for Britain", 1934. Scott was a Canadian poet
who served as Senior Chaplain for the First Canadian
Division during the First World War.

"

If it must be, let it come in the heat of action. Why flinch? It is by far the noblest form in which death can come. It is in a sense almost a privilege...

"

ALAN SEEGER

This extract comes from a letter written by Seeger, an American poet serving in the French Foreign Legion, from the Western Front in 1915.

"

Good-bye-ee! good-bye-ee!
Wipe the tear, baby dear,
   from your eye-ee.
Tho' it's hard to part I know,
I'll be tickled to death to go.
Don't cry-ee! Don't sigh-ee!
There's a silver lining in the sky-ee.

"

RP WESTON AND BERT LEE

From the popular First World War song "Good-bye-ee!".
Weston and Lee were inspired to write it after watching
factory girls calling out goodbye to soldiers marching
to London's Victoria Station.

Generally regarded as Australia's finest war poet, Leon Gellert (1892–1977) landed at Gallipoli with the 10th Battalion in April 1915.

He survived nine weeks before being injured by shrapnel and developing dysentery and septicaemia.

Sent to England to convalesce, he wrote many of his poems while there, including "The Last to Leave".

66

I heard the epics of a thousand trees,
A thousand waves I heard; and
then I knew
The waves were very old, the trees
were wise:
The dead would be remembered
evermore –
The valiant dead that gazed upon the
skies,
And slept in great battalions by
the shore.

99

LEON GELLERT

From "The Last to Leave", 1917

A successful writer of comedy verse, Jessie Pope (1868–1941) became famous for her pro-war poems that were a rallying cry to encourage enlistment.

Her poems romanticized war and are today considered jingoistic, though her views were very popular at the time.

Wilfred Owen famously dedicated his harrowing poem "Dulce et Decorum Est" to her – although he subsequently removed the dedication.

66

Come along, lads –
But you'll come on all right –
For there's only one course to pursue,
Your country is up to her neck
  in a fight,
And she's looking and calling for you.

99

JESSIE POPE

From "Who's for the Game?", 1915

66

Ip 'urrah!
Give Fritz the chuck.
Good ol' bloody Yorks!
Good-luck!
Cheer! …

…I cannot cheer or speak
Lest my voice, my heart
must break.

99

ROBERT NICHOLS

From "Eve of Assault: Infantry Going Down to Trenches".
Nichols fought at the Battle of the Somme and was
invalided home with shell shock.

"

Tales of great war and strong hearts
   wrung,
Of clash of arms, of council's brawl,
Of beauty that must early fall,
Of battle hate and battle joy…

…And now the fight begins again
The old war-joy, the old war-pain.
Sons of one school across the sea
We have no fear to fight –.

99

CHARLES HAMILTON SORLEY

From "I have not brought my Odyssey", 1916.
Sorley was killed in action in 1915 and his poems were
published posthumously.

"

A keen-edged sword, a soldier's heart
Is greater than a poet's art.
And greater than a poet's fame
A little grave that has no name.

"

FRANCIS LEDWIDGE

Killed in action at Ypres, 1917

Father Devas, a Roman Catholic chaplain, was the first on the scene after poet Francis Ledwidge (1887–1917) was killed at Ypres.

That night, he wrote in his diary, "Crowds at Holy Communion. Arranged for service but washed out by rain and fatigues. Walk in rain with dogs. Ledwidge killed, blown to bits; at Confession yesterday and Mass and Holy Communion this morning. RIP."

CHAPTER

3

WITNESS

Celebrated American poet
Walt Whitman served as a volunteer
nurse during the country's civil war.
The horror he witnessed worked its
way into poems such as "the Wound
Dresser", with injured soldiers
described in often graphic detail.

In the First World War, as the
initial wave of patriotic fervour
died down, soldier poets sought
to expose the misery of warfare,
portraying the mud, blood and filth
of the trenches, as well as the
emotional trauma of battle.

During the American Civil War, poet Walt Whitman (1819–92) estimated that he tended around 100,000 patients in his role as a volunteer nurse.

He wrote letters for them, brought them candy and fruit – and, as his poetry shows, tended the seriously wounded and dying.

"

I dress the perforated shoulder,
the foot with the bullet-wound,
Cleanse the one with a gnawing
 and putrid gangrene…
While the attendant stands behind
 aside me holding the tray and pail.

"

WALT WHITMAN
From "The Wound-Dresser", 1865

66

If you want the old battalion,
We know where they are
– Hanging on the old
barbed wire.

99

First World War song

"

A singer once, I now am fain
  to weep.
Within my soul I feel strange
  music swell,
Vast chants of tragedy
  too deep – too deep
For my poor lips to tell.

"

LESLIE COULSON

Killed in action at the Battle of Le Transloy, 1916

At the start of the Second World War, First World War veteran and poet Herbert Read (1893–1968) wrote "To a Conscript in 1940" – an imaginary meeting between two soldiers from two different conflicts.

66

A soldier passed me in the freshly
    fallen snow,
His footsteps muffled,
    his face unearthly grey:
And my heart gave a sudden leap
As I gazed on a ghost of
    five-and-twenty years ago…

…He turned towards me and I said:
'I am one of those who went
    before you
Five-and-twenty years ago: one
    of the many who never returned,
Of the many who returned and yet
    were dead.'

99

HERBERT READ

From "To a Conscript of 1940", 1940

"

In April, 1918, when on a daylight 'contact' patrol with two of my men, we suddenly confronted, round some mound or excavation, a German patrol of the same strength…
I waved a weary hand, as if to say: What is the use of killing each other? The German officer seemed to understand, and both parties turned and made their way back to their own trenches.

"

HERBERT READ

Annals of Innocence and Experience, 1940

"

Cover him, cover him soon!
And with thick-set
Masses of memoried flowers –
Hide that red wet
Thing I must somehow forget.

"

IVOR GURNEY

From "To His Love", 1917.
Already mentally fragile, Gurney was gassed and
traumatized by the war. He spent the last 15 years of
his life in asylums.

"

The wheels lurched over sprawled dead
But pained them not, though their
    bones crunched,
Their shut mouths made no moan.
They lie there huddled, friend
    and foeman,
Man born of man, and born of woman,
And shells go crying over them
From night till night and now.

"

ISAAC ROSENBERG

From "Dead Man's Dump", 1922

66

Winter has found its way into the trenches at last, but I will assure you, and leave to your imagination, the transport of delight with which we welcomed its coming. Winter is not the least of the horrors of war.

99

ISAAC ROSENBERG

From a letter to Laurence Binyon, 1916

"

The general impression in my mind is of a nightmare. We have been in the most bitter of fights. For seventeen days and seventeen nights none of us have had our clothes off, nor our boots even, except occasionally. In all that time while I was awake, gunfire… never ceased for sixty seconds… And behind it all was the constant background of the sights of the dead, the wounded, the maimed…

"

JOHN McCRAE

The Canadian poet descibes the Battle of Ypres
in a letter to his mother, 1917

❝

Cuinchy bred rats. They came up
from the canal, fed on the plentiful
corpses, and multiplied exceedingly.
While I stayed here with the Welsh,
a new officer joined the company…
When he turned in that night, he
heard a scuffling, shone his torch on
the bed, and found two rats on his
blanket tussling for the possession
of a severed hand.

❞

ROBERT GRAVES

From *Goodbye to All That*, 1929

Widely regarded as the foremost poet of the First World War, Wilfred Owen (1893–1918) did not flinch from the horror of battle in his poetry. "Dulce et Decorum Est" has an unambiguous anti-war message, immersing the reader in a horrifying depiction of the aftermath of a gas attack.

Owen was killed in action in November 1918, just one week before the Armistice. Virtually unknown as a poet in his lifetime, most of his poems were published posthumously.

"

If you could hear, at every jolt, the blood
Come gargling from the froth-corrupted
   lungs,
Obscene as cancer, bitter as the cud
Of vile, incurable sores on innocent
   tongues,—
My friend, you would not tell with such
   high zest
To children ardent for some desperate glory,
The old Lie: *Dulce et decorum est
   Pro patria mori.*

"

WILFRED OWEN

From "Dulce et Decorum Est", describing the aftermath
of a gas attack, 1918. The Latin in the final two lines means
"It is sweet and fitting to die for one's country".

66

I suppose I can endure cold, and
fatigue, and the face-to-face death,
as well as another; but extra for
me there is the universal pervasion
of Ugliness. Hideous landscapes,
vile noises, foul language, even
from one's own mouth (for all are
devil ridden)…

…Everything is unnatural, broken, blasted; the distortion of the dead, whose unburiable bodes sit outside the dug-outs all day, all night, the most execrable sights on earth. In poetry we call them the most glorious, but to sit with them all day, all night… and a week later to come back and find them still sitting there in motionless groups. THAT is what saps the 'soldierly spirit'.

"

WILFRED OWEN

In a letter to his mother, 4 February 1917

One of the leading poets of the First World War, Siegfried Sassoon (1886–1967) was wounded in 1917.

After publishing an open letter in *The Times*, in which he claimed the war was being deliberately prolonged by the government, he was sent to Craiglockhart War Hospital in Edinburgh where he met Wilfred Owen – who was recovering from shell shock.

Sassoon would have a profound influence on Owen, and on his poetry.

"

O Jesus, make it stop!

"

SIEGFRIED SASSOON

From "Attack", 1918

Canadian poet Frank Prewett
(1893–1962) served in both the
First and Second World Wars.

In early 1916, an explosion caused
severe back injuries, whilst in 1918,
he was buried alive under a collapsed
dugout and had to claw his way to
the surface.

While receiving treatment for
shell shock, he met and formed
a deep attachment to Siegfried
Sassoon.

66

Hearing the whine and crash
We hastened out
And found a few poor men
Lying about.

I put my hand in the breast
Of the first met.
His heart thumped, stopped, and I drew
My hand out wet.

99

FRANK PREWETT

From "The Card Game", 1924

Chilean poet Pablo Neruda (1904–73) was living in Spain when the Spanish Civil War broke out.

The assassination of his close friend García Lorca, along with other atrocities, led him to write *Spain in Our Hearts*, a collection of poetry showing solidarity with the Republican side of the conflict.

He became known for his lyrical poetry shot through with haunting imagery about the "pus and pestilence" of the war.

66

And one morning it was all
   burning,
and one morning bonfires
sprang out of the earth
devouring humans…

99

PABLO NERUDA

From "I'm Explaining a Few Things", 1937

"

Eyes of men thinking, hoping,
    waiting
Eyes of men loving, cursing,
    hating
The eyes of the wounded sodden
    in red
The eyes of the dying and those
    of the dead.

"

ANONYMOUS

Lines discovered in an International Brigadier's notebook,
mid-1930s

"

Still falls the Rain –
Dark as the world of man, black
   as our loss –
Blind as the nineteen and
   hundred and forty nails
Upon the Cross.

"

EDITH SITWELL

From "Still Falls the Rain" (The Raids, 1940,
Night and Dawn)

Philosopher Theodor Adorno (1903–69) stated that "to write poetry after Auschwitz is barbaric."

His point was that any attempt to depict the experience of those who lived and died in Nazi ghettoes and concentration camps somehow diminished their suffering.

However, many survivors and their descendants have used poetry to provide a window into a period that is very difficult to comprehend, and as a way to cope with their trauma.

"

My stomach complains and
I mumble quietly to myself:
To eat? Not to eat?
It is such a small piece of
bread after all.

"

PETR KEST

Written on a scrap of paper in the Bergen-Belsen
concentration camp by 10-year-old Petr Kest, 1944

66

First they came for the socialists,
and I did not speak out –
because I was not a socialist.

Then they came for the trade unionists,
and I did not speak out –
because I was not a trade unionist.

Then they came for the Jews,
and I did not speak out –
because I was not a Jew.

Then they came for me – and there
was no one left to speak for me.

99

PASTOR MARTIN NIEMÖLLER

Niemöller, a German Lutheran pastor, was arrested in 1937
and spent seven years in concentration camps. After his release,
he preached collective guilt for Nazi persecution and crimes
against humanity.

"

Never shall I forget that smoke.
Never shall I forget the small faces
of the children whose bodies
I saw transformed into smoke
under a silent sky.

"

ELIE WIESEL

From "Never Shall I Forget", 1958.
A concentration camp survivor, Wiesel made it his life's
work to bear witness to the genocide committed by the
Nazis during the Second World War.

In June 1944, Carentan was a peaceful French town that became the scene of some of the most ferocious fighting in the Battle for Normandy.

Parachutists with the US 101st Airborne Division landed nearby and fought house to house with Nazi troops – amongst them was poet Louis Simpson (1923–2012), a Jamaican immigrant who wrote the poem "Carentan O Carentan".

"

Everything's all right, Mother
Everyone gets the same
At one time or another.
It's all in the game…

Carentan O Carentan
Before we met with you
We never yet had lost a man
Or known what death could do.

"

LOUIS SIMPSON

From "Carentan O Carentan", 1949

Keith Douglas (1920–44) commanded a tank troop in North Africa where he wrote poetry about his experiences.

Despite the carnage he witnessed, he developed a detached and unsentimental tone, and shied away from making any political point. He took part in the D-Day landings on 6 June 1944, and was in one of the first Allied units to enter Bayeux.

Three days later, he was killed by a mortar shell near Caen, at the age of 24.

"

Now in my dial of glass appears
The soldier who is going to die.
He smiles, and moves about in ways
His mother knows, habits of his…

"

KEITH DOUGLAS

From "How to Kill", 1943

CHAPTER

4

THE PITY OF WAR

THROUGH WAR POETRY, WE MAY LEARN
OF PRIDE AND PATRIOTISM, OF COURAGE
AND CAMARADERIE AND OF SUFFERING
AND DEATH. HOWEVER, IT IS THE PITY OF
WAR — THE LOSS OF HUMAN VALUES
— THAT PERHAPS DISTURBS US MOST.

WILFRED OWEN FAMOUSLY WROTE,
"MY SUBJECT IS WAR, AND THE PITY OF
WAR. THE POETRY IS IN THE PITY..."
HIS AIM WAS NOT LYRICAL BEAUTY,
NOR DID HE WISH TO GRATUITOUSLY
DWELL ON WAR'S HORRORS. INSTEAD,
HE WANTED TO EXPOSE WAR AS AN EVIL
COMMITTED AGAINST HUMANITY ITSELF.

"

I was in the midst of it all –
saw war where war is worst –
not on the battlefields, no –
in the hospitals... there I mixed
with it: and now I say
God damn the wars – all wars:
God damn every war:
God damn 'em! God damn 'em!

"

WALT WHITMAN

The American poet served as a volunteer nurse in the
American Civil War, 1888

66

O God! That whole damned war business is about nine hundred and ninety-nine parts diarrhoea to one part glory: the people who like the wars should be compelled to fight the wars: they are hellish business, wars – all wars.

99

WALT WHITMAN
1888

Already a major novelist, Thomas Hardy (1840–1928) transformed himself into a major war poet at the outset of the 20th century. He wrote several poems about the South African Boer War, including "Drummer Hodge".

In 1914, his poem "Men Who March Away" captured the early enthusiasm of the war, when a quick victory seemed certain: "What of the faith and fire within us / Men who march away?"

"

They throw in Drummer Hodge, to rest
Uncoffined — just as found:
His landmark is a kopje-crest
That breaks the veldt around:
And foreign constellations west
Each night above his mound.

"

THOMAS HARDY

From "Drummer Hodge", 1899

Maresuke Nogi (1849–1912) commanded Japanese troops during the Russo-Japanese War of 1905 and became one of the heroes of the campaign.

One of his most famous war poems is "Outside the Goldland Fortress", which was learned by generations of schoolchildren.

Nogi spent his entire adult life in service to the emperor – and committed suicide on the day of his funeral.

"

A foul, blood-soaked wind
Over a fresh battlefield.
The horses do not stir,
The men do not speak.
In the slanted rays of
   the setting sun,
Outside the Fortress at Goldland.

"

MARESUKE NOGI

From "Outside the Goldland Fortress", 1905

"

Today, as I rode by,
I saw the brown leaves dropping
    from their tree...

And wandered slowly thence
For thinking of a gallant multitude
Which now all withering lay,
Slain by no wind of age or pestilence,
But in their beauty strewed
Like snowflakes falling on the
    Flemish clay.

"

MARGARET POSTGATE

"The Falling Leaves", 1915. This was one of the first anti-
war poems written from a women's perspective.

"

Oh guns of France, oh guns of France,
Be still, you crash in vain…
Heavily up the south wind throb
Dull dreams of pain…

Oh we'll lie quite still, not listen
    nor look,
While the earth's bounds reel and
    shake,
Lest, battered too long, our walls
    and we
Should break… should break…

"

ROSE MACAULAY

From "Picnic: July 1917"

"

This book is not about heroes.
English poetry is not yet fit to speak
of them. Nor is it about deeds, or
lands, nor anything about glory,
honour, might, majesty, dominion,
or power, except War. Above all
I am not concerned with Poetry.
My subject is War, and the pity of
War. The Poetry is in the pity.

"

WILFRED OWEN

From the preface to a poetry collection sketched out before
his death in November 1918

Siegfred Sassoon's "Suicide in the Trenches" (1918) sharply contrasts with the romanticized perspectives offered by poets such as Rupert Brooke and Jessie Pope:

"

You smug-faced crowds with
    kindling eye
Who cheer when soldier lads march by,
Sneak home and pray you'll
    never know
The hell where youth and laughter go.

"

In 1917, Robert Graves (1895–1985) wrote a letter in which he beseeched fellow poet Wilfred Owen to rise above his misery:

"For God's sake cheer up and write more optimistically – the war's not ended yet but a poet should have a spirit above wars."

Wilfred Owen is thought to have responded by writing "Apologia Pro Poemate Meo", which means "In defence of my poetry".

66

You shall not hear their mirth:
You shall not come to think them
    well content
By any jest of mine. These men
    are worth
Your tears: You are not worth
    their merriment.

99

WILFRED OWEN

From "Apologia Pro Poemate Meo"
("In defence of my poetry"), 1917

Vera Brittain (1893–1970) was an English author, poet, feminist and pacifist best known for her memoir *Testament of Youth*, which chronicles her experiences as a nurse during the First World War.

As well as the trauma of witnessing and treating severely wounded soldiers, she suffered tragic personal losses, including the deaths of her fiancé, Roland Leighton, and brother, Edward.

"

Your battle-wounds are scars
    upon my heart,
Received when in that grand
    and tragic "show"
You played your part
    Two years ago…

"

VERA BRITTAIN

From "To My Brother", written to commemorate
the bravery of her brother, Edward, at the Battle of
the Somme, for which he won the Military Cross.
He was killed on the Italian Front in 1918.

66

I used to talk of the Beauty
of War; but it is only War in
the abstract that is beautiful.
Modern warfare is merely
a trade…

99

ROLAND LEIGHTON

In a letter to his fiancée, Vera Brittain, 2 August 1915.
He died from a sniper wound a few months later,
at the age of 20.

"

Violets from Plug Street Wood,
Sweet, I send you oversea.
(It is strange they should be blue,
Blue, when his soaked blood was red…)

Think what they have meant to me –
Life and hope and Love and You
(and you did not see them grow
Where his mangled body lay
Hiding horrors from the day;
Sweetest, it was better so.)

"

ROLAND LEIGHTON

From "Villanelle", a poem sent to his fiancée,
Vera Brittain, 1915

May Wedderburn Cannan produced three volumes of poetry during and after the First World War.

Her most famous war poem is "Rouen", which has become the most anthologized poem by a woman from the conflict. She worked as a volunteer in the railhead canteen at Rouen, which provided food and coffee to troops arriving in France and travelling on by train to the Front.

❝

Quiet night-time over Rouen, and
    the station full of soldiers,
All the youth and pride of England
    from the ends of all the earth;
And the rifles piled together, and the
    creaking of the sword-belts,
And the faces bent above them, and
    the gay, heart-breaking mirth.

❞

MAY WEDDERBURN CANNAN

From "Rouen", 1917

"In Flanders Fields", where "the poppies blow / Between the crosses, row on row" quickly came to symbolize the sacrifices of all those fighting in the First World War.

Its author, John McCrae (1872–1918), was a Canadian doctor and teacher who began writing poetry as a young boy. One of 45,000 Canadians to join up when war was declared, he served as a medical officer, tending hundreds of injured soldiers every day.

John McCrae fell ill with pneumonia in January 1918. He died later that month – after learning he had been appointed consulting physician to the First British Army, the first Canadian to achieve this honour.

He was buried with full military honours in Wimereux Cemetery, just north of Boulogne, not far from the fields of Flanders. His much-loved horse, Bonfire, led the procession.

Vernon Scannell (1922–2007) was seriously wounded in the 1944 Normandy landings. His poem "The Great War" describes how when war is mentioned, it is the powerful, haunting images of the First World War rather than any other that spring to mind:

66

Duckboards, mud and rats.
Then, like patrols, tunes creep into
    the mind:
A long, long trail,
    The Rose of No Man's Land,
Home Fires and Tipperary…

…And I remember,
Not the war I fought in
But the one called Great
Which ended in a sepia November
Four years before my birth.

99

VERNON SCANNELL

From "The Great War", 1962

Miguel Hernández (1910–1942) broke free from the poverty and deprivation of his childhood to become one of Spain's best-loved poets.

During the Spanish Civil War, he served in the Republican Army – and was sentenced to death by Franco at the end of the war, in 1939.

He died in prison three years later, aged 31. His war poems are amongst his finest work.

"

The train wet with flowing blood,
the fragile train of those who
    bleed,
the silent, the painful, the pale,
the train hushed with suffering…

"

MIGUEL HERNÁNDEZ

From "Train of the Wounded", 1939

66

In the nightmare of the dark
All the dogs of Europe bark,
And the living nations wait,
Each sequestered in its hate…

99

WH AUDEN

From "Another Time", 1940

"

That is what War is,
I thought: two ships pass
each other, and nobody
waves his hand.

"

CHRISTOPHER ISHERWOOD

From *Journey to a War*, 1939

"

But darkness opens like a knife
   for you
And you are marked down by your
   pulsing brain
And isolated
And your breathing
Your breathing is the blast, the bullet
And the final sky

"

LAURIE LEE

From "Spanish Frontier", *A Moment of War*, 1937

66

I am constantly amazed by
man's inhumanity to man.

99

PRIMO LEVI

From *If This Is a Man*, 1947

John Gillespie Magee, a Royal Canadian Air Force pilot, was killed in a plane crash over Lincolnshire, England, in 1941.

His sonnet "High Flight" is an ode to the joys of being a pilot, describing the almost spiritual feeling of flying high above the clouds.

It became so popular that it was used on many of the gravestones at Virginia's Arlington National Cemetery in the US.

"

Oh! I have slipped the surly bonds
of Earth
And danced the skies on laughter-
silvered wings;
Sunward I've climbed, and joined
the tumbling mirth
of sun-split clouds,—and done a
hundred things
You have not dreamed of—wheeled
and soared and swung
High in the sunlit silence…

"

JOHN GILLESPIE MAGEE

From 'High Flight", 1941

"The Butterfly", one of the most famous poems to emerge from the Second World War, was written by Jewish-Czechoslovakian poet Pavel Friedmann (1921–44) at Theresienstadt concentration camp.

In September 1944, he was deported to Auschwitz where he died at the age of 23.

66

For seven weeks I've lived in here,
Penned up inside this ghetto
But I have found my people here.
The dandelions call to me
And the white chestnut candles in
the court.
Only I never saw another butterfly.

99

PAVEL FRIEDMANN

From "The Butterfly", 4 June 1942

Amateur poet Takijirō Ōnishi (1891–1945) served as an admiral in the Imperial Japanese Navy during the Second World War, eventually becoming head of the Naval Aviation Development Division.

He developed the technique for suicide "kamikaze" air attacks, and often gave his pilots short verses written in the style of traditional Japanese calligraphy – such as the one shown opposite.

Following Japan's surrender in 1945, he committed ritual seppuku in his quarters, dying of self-inflicted wounds.

"

Today in flower,
Tomorrow scattered by the
    wind –
Such is our blossom life.
How can we think its
    fragrance lasts forever?

"

TAKIJIRŌ ŌNISHI

Poem presented to Japanese troops before they carried
out a kamikaze attack, 1945

Langston Hughes (1901–67) was
a prominent American poet, novelist
and activist who wrote about the
experiences of African Americans and
their struggles for equality.

While he did not directly experience
war, he wrote several poems that reflect
on its impact upon society.

In "Wisdom and War" he muses
on how apathy and stupidity are the
catalysts for war.

66

To think
Is much against
The will.
Better–
And easier–
To kill.

99

LANGSTON HUGHES

From "Wisdom and War", 1943

A mathematics teacher before the Second World War, British poet John Jarmain (1911–44) first saw action at the Battle of Alamein – which gave rise to one of his most famous poems.

He was killed in Normandy several weeks after the 1944 D-Day landings and is buried in the 6th Airborne Cemetery at Ranville.

His poems, which he sent to his wife in numbered airmails, were published to critical acclaim after the war.

66

There are flowers now, they say,
    at Alamein;
Yes, flowers in the minefields now.
So those that come to view that
    vacant scene,
Where death remains and agony
    has been
Will find the lilies grow –
Flowers, and nothing that we know.

99

JOHN JARMAIN

From "El Almein", 1942

English poet Sidney Keyes (1922–43)
joined the British Army in 1942.
He was sent to Tunisia in 1943, where
he was killed in action just three weeks
later, at the age of 20.

Remembered for his powerful war
poetry, which captures the experiences
of soldiers on the front lines,
he was awarded the Hawthornden
Prize posthumously in 1944.

"

I am the man who looked for
   peace and found
My own eyes barbed.
I am the man who groped
   for words and found,
An arrow in my hand.

"

SIDNEY KEYES

From "War Poet", 1943

"Facing It", a poem by Yusef Komunyakaa (born 1947), is about a visit by a war veteran to the Vietnam Veterans Memorial in Washington, DC.

Seeing his own reflection in the polished black granite, the narrator is forced to confront his memories of the war and the people he lost.

The poem also subtly reflects the tense racial backdrop of the Vietnam War, when many black Americans fought for a country that continued to treat them as second-class citizens.

“

My black face fades,
hiding inside the black granite.
I said I wouldn't,
dammit: No tears.
I'm stone. I'm flesh.

”

YUSEF KOMUNYAKAA

From "Facing It", 1984

CHAPTER

5

DEATH'S KINGDOM

WHETHER EXTOLLING THE HEROISM OF
THE WAR DEAD, EXPOSING THE BRUTALITY
OF DEATH IN BATTLE, OR EVOKING THE
GRIEF AND SUFFERING OF THOSE LEFT
BEHIND, WAR POETRY IS INEVITABLY
CONCERNED WITH THE THEME OF DEATH.

FROM HORACE'S "IT IS SWEET AND
GLORIOUS TO DIE FOR ONE'S COUNTRY"
TO THE ROMANTICIZED VIEW OF DEATH
IN ALAN SEEGER'S "RENDEZVOUS WITH
DEATH" OR THE HORROR EXPRESSED
IN BRIAN TURNER'S IRAQ POEM "BODY
BAGS", WE ARE REMINDED OF THE
HUMAN COST OF WAR.

66

The glorious and the decent way
  of dying
Is for one's country. Run, and
  death will seize
You no less surely. The young
  coward, flying
Gets his quietus in the back and
  the knees.

99

HORACE

From "The Odes", 23 BCE

66

Raise the Cromlech high!
MacMoghcorb is slain,
And other men's renown
Has leave to live again.

Cold at last he lies
Neath the burial-stone
All the blood he shed
Could not save his own.

99

ANONYMOUS

From "The Lament of Maev Leith-Dherg", 12th century

66

Hard the breathing rattles,
   quite glazed already the eye,
Yet life struggles hard,
(Come sweet death! be persuaded
   O beautiful death!
In mercy come quickly.)

99

WALT WHITMAN

From "The Wound Dresser", 1897

East and west on fields forgotten
Bleach the bones of comrades slain
Lovely lads and dead and rotten;
None that go return again.

AE HOUSMAN

From "A Shropshire Lad", 1896

American Alan Seeger (1888–1916)
– often compared to Rupert Brooke
because of his youthful idealism – served
with the French Foreign Legion during
the First World War.

The narrator in his famous poem
"I Have a Rendezvous with Death"
tells of his regret at leaving behind life's
pleasures, but he does not fear death –
instead, it is a matter of honour.

Seeger was killed in action in 1916.

"

But I've a rendezvous with Death
At midnight in some flaming town,
When Spring trips north again
  this year,
And I to my pledged word am true,
I shall not fail that rendezvous.

"

ALAN SEEGER

From "I Have a Rendezvous with Death", 1915

"

Have you news of my boy Jack?
Not this tide.
When d'you think that he'll
   come back?
Not with this wind blowing,
   and this tide.

"

RUDYARD KIPLING

From "My Boy Jack", 1916. Kipling wrote the poem for
Jack Cornwell, the youngest recipient of the Victoria
Cross, who died at the Battle of Jutland. Kipling lost his
own son, John, at the Battle of Loos in 1915.

"

Red lips are not so red
As the stained stones kissed
by the English dead.

"

WILFRED OWEN

From "Greater Love", written in either 1917 or 1918

On 31 July 1917, the Third Battle of
Ypres, or "Passchendaele", began.
Two thousand Allied guns opened up
on German lines and by the end of the
three-month long campaign, more than
500,000 men from both sides had been
wounded or killed.

Passchendaele has become synonymous
with horror – the men came to fear
the treacherous mud more than enemy
fire, with unknown numbers of men and
horses drowning in the quagmire.

> **I died in hell – they called it Passchendaele.**

SIEGFRIED SASSOON

From "Memorial Tablet", 1918

In November 1915, Siegfried Sassoon's younger brother, Hamo Sassoon, was killed in the Gallipoli campaign.

A few months later, David Cuthbert Thomas – with whom he is believed to have had a close relationship – was killed in France.

These deaths are thought to have inspired such poems as "The Last Meeting" and "A Letter Home".

66

I know that he is lost among
the stars,
And may return no more
but in their light.

99

SIEGFRIED SASSOON

From "The Last Meeting", 1916

British-Canadian poet Robert Service (1874–1958) worked as a war correspondent during the Balkan Wars of 1912–13.

During the First World War, he served with the American Red Cross as an ambulance driver and stretcher bearer.

His poems are noted for their straightforward, often gritty style. His poetry collection *Rhymes of a Red Cross Man* was dedicated to his brother, Albert, who was killed in action in France in August 1916.

"

Yon's Barret, the painter of
    pictures, yon carcass that rots
    on the wire;
His hand with its sensitive cunning
    is crisped to a cinder with fire;
His eyes with their magical vision
    are bubbles of glutinous mire…

"

ROBERT SERVICE

From "The Three Tommies", 1916

César Vallejo (1892–1938) was a Peruvian poet. He moved to Spain during the Spanish Civil War, where he saw the horror of the frontline with his own eyes.

An ardent supporter of the Republicans, he wrote stirring poems about Spain's tragedy. However, he would not live to see the outcome of the war, dying of a mysterious illness in 1938.

66

At the end of the battle the fighter
    lay dead. A man came to him
and said: 'Don't die! I love you
    too much!'
But the corpse, alas, went on dying.

Two came to him and again said:
'Don't leave us! Take heart!
Come back to life!'
But the corpse, alas, went on dying.

99

CÉSAR VALLEJO

From "Mass", 1937

English poet and communist John Cornford (1915–36) became the first Englishman to enlist against Franco in the Spanish Civil War. He was killed in battle on the Cordoba Front in December 1936, at the age of 21.

His poems from Spain include "A Letter from Aragon", "Full Moon at Tierz: Before The Storming of Huesca" and "A Letter to Margot Heinemann". He had met and fallen in love with fellow communist Margot while they were both studying at Cambridge University.

66

On the last mile to Huesca,
The last fence for our pride,
Think so kindly, dear, that I
Sense you at my side.

And if bad luck should lay
   my strength
Into the shallow grave,
Remember all the good you can;
Don't forget my love.

99

JOHN CORNFORD

From "To Margot Heinemann", 1936

Charles Causley (1917–2003) saw active service during the Second World War as a seaman in the Royal Navy.

The son of a Western Front soldier, who died as a result of being gassed – when his only child, Charles, was seven – Causley experienced what he described as "survivor's guilt".

Around 50 of his 270-odd poems deal directly with war, at least to some extent.

66

Draw the blanket of ocean
Over the frozen face.
He lies, his eyes quarried by
    glittering fish,
Staring through the green
    freezing sea-glass
At the Northern Lights.

99

CHARLES CAUSLEY

From "Convoy", 1951. There was a horrific loss of life
in the Allied Arctic convoys, which were sent in
treacherous conditions to the Soviet ports of Murmansk
and Archangelsk.

American poet Brian Turner (born 1967) turned his experience as a soldier in the US Army during the Iraq War into poetry.

His collection *Here, Bullet* captures the pain, confusion and disorientation of armed conflict, as well as the emotional toll it took on those who served.

It is a poignant reminder of the human cost of war.

> A murder of crows looks on in silence
> from the eucalyptus trees above
> as we stand over the bodies –
> who look as if they might roll over,
> wake from a dream and question us
> about the blood drying on their
> scalps…

BRIAN TURNER

From "Body Bags", 2005

CHAPTER

6

LEST WE FORGET

UP TO 11 MILLION SOLDIERS LOST THEIR
LIVES IN THE FIRST WORLD WAR, WHILE
MORE THAN A MILLION WERE EITHER
WOUNDED OR KILLED AT THE BATTLE OF
THE SOMME ALONE. IT IS DIFFICULT FOR
THE HUMAN MIND TO COMPUTE SUCH
SLAUGHTER – AND IT IS NO WONDER
THAT THE THEME OF REMEMBRANCE AND
HONOURING THE DEAD LOOMS LARGE IN
WAR POETRY. WHERE ORDINARY WORDS
MAY FAIL, POETRY SERVES AS A MEMORIAL
TO THE FALLEN – AND AS A WARNING TO
FUTURE GENERATIONS.

"

All a poet can do today is warn. That is why the true Poets must be truthful.

"

WILFRED OWEN

From the preface to a poetry collection sketched out before his death in November 1918

66

When you go home,
tell them of us and say,
for their tomorrow we gave
our today.

99

JOHN MAXWELL EDMONDS

Written during the First World War.
The words form the epitaph in the war cemetery in
Kohima, commemorating the fallen of the Battle of
Kohima in April 1944.

One of the best-known war poems, "For the Fallen" was written at the onset of the First World War – and is still read at Remembrance Sunday services today.

The author was Laurence Binyon (1869–1943), a poet, dramatist and art scholar. At the time of writing, he was too old to enlist and had never been to the Western Front – though he later volunteered in British hospital for French soldiers.

> **"**
> They shall grow not old,
>   as we that are left grow old:
> Age shall not weary them,
>   nor the years condemn.
> At the going down of the sun
>   and in the morning
> We will remember them.
> **"**

LAURENCE BINYON

From "For the Fallen", published in *The Times*,
September 1914

The well-known line "lest we forget", often used in war remembrance services, first appeared in a Rudyard Kipling poem called "Recessional".

It was written for Queen Victoria's Diamond Jubilee in 1897, with almost all of the poem's stanzas ending with the line, "Lest we forget – lest we forget!"

The poem can be seen as a prayer for the British Empire, which at the time was under threat.

> **"**
> Lord God of Hosts,
> be with us yet,
> Lest we forget –
> lest we forget!
> **"**

RUDYARD KIPLING

"Recessional", 1897

"

When we forget those heroes,
When we withhold our hand,
May shame be ours forever,
All shame on this our land.
And so we yield them homage
Upon this solemn day,
And to those men of Anzac
Our debt of honour pay.

"

LE HOMFRAY

From "Our Debt of Honour", 1921

66

I think it better that in times like these
A poet's mouth be silent, for in truth
We have no gift to set a
    statesman right;
He has had enough of meddling who
    can please
A young girl in the indolence of
    her youth,
Or an old man upon a winter's night.

99

WB YEATS

"On Being Asked for a War Poem", 1915

"

Peace, so precious, must be bought with blood and tears. These are the men who pay the price. Come let us honour them, aye, and envy them the manner of their dying for not all the jewelled orders on the breasts of the living can vie in glory with the little wooden crosses the humblest of these has won.

"

ROBERT SERVICE

Reporting from the Western Front for the *Toronto Star*, 18 December 1915

> **❝**
> # Their name liveth for evermore.
> **❞**

A phrase from the King James Version of the Bible,
forming the second half of a line in Ecclesiasticus or Sirach,
chapter 44, verse 14.

It has been widely inscribed on war memorials
since the First World War.

The link between poppies and war remembrance dates from the Napoleonic wars.

It was noted that poppies grew abundantly on battlefields – and a connection was made between the blood-red colour of the flowers and the blood of fallen soldiers.

The association between poppies and fallen soldiers was popularized during the First World War and is especially evident in John McCrae's poem "In Flanders Fields".

"

We are the Dead. Short days ago
We lived, felt dawn, saw sunset glow,
Loved, and were loved, and now
    we lie
In Flanders Fields.

"

JOHN MCCRAE
"In Flanders Fields", 1915

"

And my last words shall be these – that it is only from the inmost silences of the heart that we know the world for what it is, and ourselves for what the world has made us.

"

SIEGFRIED SASSOON,

Sherston's Progress, 1936

66

The opposite of love is not hate, it's indifference.

99

ELIE WIESEL

Writer, poet and concentration camp survivor, who made it his life's work to speak out against the atrocities committed by the Nazis in the Second World War.

66

What passing bells for these
  who die as cattle?
– Only the monstrous anger of
  the guns.
Only the stuttering rifles' rapid
  rattle
Can patter out their hasty
  orisons…

99

WILFRED OWEN

From "Anthem for Doomed Youth", 1922

"

Go tell those old men,
safe in bed,
We took their orders
and are dead.

"

AD HOPE

From "Inscription for a War", 1940

In the poem "Poppies", British poet Jane Weir poignantly explores the themes of remembrance, grief and loss from a mother's perspective:

"

On reaching the top of the hill
    I traced the inscriptions on the
    war memorial…

…I listened, hoping to hear
    your playground voice catching
    on the wind.

"

In "Times of Peace", poet John Agard powerfully reminds us that although veterans are no longer fighting a physical battle, they are still "fighting" as they attempt to adapt to everyday life and escape the horrors of war:

66

And what of hearts in times of
    peace?
Will war-worn hearts grow sluggish
like Valentine roses wilting
without the adrenalin of a bullet's
    blood-rush?

99

66

Do you remember that hour of din
    before the attack –
And the anger, the blind compassion
    that seized and shook you then…?

Have you forgotten yet?…
Look up, and swear by the green
    of the spring that you'll
      never forget!

99

SIEGFRIED SASSOON

From "Aftermath", March 1919

THE LITTLE BOOK OF
BIBLE VERSES

Published in 2024 by OH!
An Imprint of Welbeck Non-Fiction Limited,
part of Welbeck Publishing Group.
Offices in: London – 20 Mortimer Street, London W1T 3JW
and Sydney – Level 17, 207 Kent St, Sydney NSW 2000 Australia
www.welbeckpublishing.com

ISBN 978-1-80069-563-4

All bible verses quoted are taken from the King James Version
Compiled and written by: Victoria Denne
Project manager: Russell Porter
Production: Jess Brisley

A CIP catalogue record for this book is available from the British Library

Printed in China

10 9 8 7 6 5 4 3 2 1

THE LITTLE BOOK OF
BIBLE VERSES

WORDS OF INSPIRATION
FOR EVERY OCCASION

CONTENTS

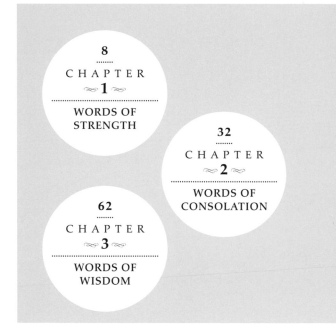

INTRODUCTION

In addition to being the founding document of Christianity, the Bible contains some of the most beautiful writing ever committed to page. Much like the works of Shakespeare, it is hard to overstate the influence this text has had purely from a literary standpoint, even before we consider its profound religious and spiritual significance.

Over the centuries countless individuals across the globe have turned to scripture in times of strife, and it could be argued that its words of strength and encouragement are needed now more than ever, as the world is at war once again and the threat of climate change looms, ever-present.

In *The Little Book of Bible Verses*, you will find some of our favourite words of scripture, for every time of life and every stop on the journey, whether it be testing or triumphant; words to give you strength in adversity, consolation in times of grief, hope in seemingly hopeless situations, and wisdom in uncertain times. There are also verses of motivation when you need just that little extra push, and not forgetting those that will spark joy when celebration is called for.

Because, as the book of Ecclesiastes says: "To every thing there is a season, and a time to every purpose under the heaven: A time to be born, and a time to die... A time to weep, and a time to laugh; a time to mourn, and a time to dance..." And just as there is a time for every thing, there is almost surely a Bible verse to go with it.

CHAPTER

1

WORDS OF STRENGTH

When your problems feel insurmountable, let these verses inspire strength and fortitude in the face of weakness.

66

My grace is
sufficient for thee:
for my strength is
made perfect
in weakness.

99

2 Corinthians 12:9

My flesh and my
heart faileth: but
God is the strength
of my heart, and my
portion forever.

Psalm 73:26

Be strong and of a
good courage, fear not,
nor be afraid of them:
for the Lord thy God, he
it is that doth go with
thee; he will not fail thee,
nor forsake thee.

Deuteronomy 31:6

God is in the midst
of her; she shall not
be moved: God shall
help her, and that
right early.

Psalm 46:5

> **I can do all things through Christ which strengtheneth me.**

Philippians 4:13

God, thou art terrible out of thy holy places: the God of Israel is he that giveth strength and power unto his people. Blessed be God.

Psalm 68:35

The Lord is my strength and
my shield; my heart trusted
in him, and I am helped:
therefore my heart greatly
rejoiceth; and with my song
will I praise him.

Psalm 28:7

The Lord is my light
and my salvation;
whom shall I fear?
the Lord is the strength
of my life; of whom
shall I be afraid?

Psalm 27:1

66

Watch ye, stand fast in the faith, quit you like men, be strong.

99

1 Corinthians 16:13

But they that wait upon
the Lord shall renew their
strength; they shall mount
up with wings as eagles;
they shall run, and not be
weary; and they shall walk,
and not faint.

Isaiah 40:31

Now the God
of patience and
consolation grant
you to be likeminded
one toward another
according to
Christ Jesus…

Romans 15:5

66

Have not I commanded
thee? Be strong and of
a good courage; be not
afraid, neither be thou
dismayed: for the Lord
thy God is with thee
whithersoever thou goest.

99

Joshua 1:9

God is our refuge and
strength, a very present help
in trouble. Therefore will not
we fear, though the earth
be removed, and though the
mountains be carried into
the midst of the sea; Though
the waters thereof roar and
be troubled, though the
mountains shake with the
swelling thereof.

Psalm 46:1–3

> **"**
>
> Ah Lord God! behold,
> thou hast made the
> heaven and the earth
> by thy great power and
> stretched out arm, and
> there is nothing too
> hard for thee..
>
> **"**

Jeremiah 32:17

Seek the Lord, and his strength: seek his face evermore.

Psalm 105:4

66

The Lord is my strength
and song, and he is become
my salvation: he is my God,
and I will prepare him an
habitation; my father's God,
and I will exalt him.

99

Exodus 15:2

> ❝
> He giveth power to
> the faint; and to them
> that have no might he
> increaseth strength.
> ❞

Isaiah 40:29

The Lord will give strength unto his people; the Lord will bless his people with peace.

Psalm 29:11

But the Lord is
faithful, who shall
stablish you, and
keep you from evil.

2 Thessalonians 3:3

“

Therefore I take pleasure
in infirmities, in reproaches,
in necessities, in persecutions,
in distresses for Christ's sake:
for when I am weak, then
am I strong.

”

2 Corinthians 12:10

The Lord God is my
strength, and he will make
my feet like hinds' feet, and
he will make me to walk
upon mine high places.
To the chief singer on my
stringed instruments.

Habakkuk 3:19

> Finally, my brethren, be strong in the Lord, and in the power of his might.

Ephesians 6:10

CHAPTER

2

WORDS OF CONSOLATION

Grief and despair come to us all at one time or another. When they do, let these words uplift your spirit and soothe your soul.

My soul melteth
for heaviness:
strengthen thou
me according
unto thy word.

Psalm 119:28

But I will sing of thy
power; yea, I will sing
aloud of thy mercy in the
morning: for thou hast
been my defence and
refuge in the day of
my trouble.

Psalm 59:16

Then he said unto them,
Go your way, eat the fat, and
drink the sweet, and send
portions unto them for whom
nothing is prepared: for this day
is holy unto our Lord: neither be
ye sorry; for the joy of the
Lord is your strength.

Nehemiah 8:10

66

Fear thou not; for I am
with thee: be not dismayed;
for I am thy God: I will
strengthen thee; yea, I will
help thee; yea, I will uphold
thee with the right hand of
my righteousness.

99

Isaiah 41:10

But the God of all
grace, who hath called
us unto his eternal glory
by Christ Jesus, after
that ye have suffered a
while, make you perfect,
stablish, strengthen,
settle you.

1 Peter 5:10

> Blessed are they that mourn: for they shall be comforted.

Matthew 5:4

And God shall wipe away
all tears from their eyes; and
there shall be no more death,
neither sorrow, nor crying,
neither shall there be any
more pain: for the former
things are passed away.

Revelation 21:4

He healeth the broken in heart, and bindeth up their wounds.

Psalm 147:3

Casting all your care upon him; for he careth for you.

1 Peter 5:7

The Lord is nigh
unto them that are of
a broken heart; and
saveth such as be of a
contrite spirit.

Psalm 34:18

Peace I leave with you, my peace I give unto you: not as the world giveth, give I unto you. Let not your heart be troubled, neither let it be afraid.

John 14:27

Come unto me, all ye that
labour and are heavy laden,
and I will give you rest. Take
my yoke upon you, and learn
of me; for I am meek and
lowly in heart: and ye shall
find rest unto your souls.
For my yoke is easy, and my
burden is light.

Matthew 11:28–30

> **"**
>
> Trust in the Lord with
> all thine heart; and lean
> not unto thine own
> understanding. In all thy
> ways acknowledge him, and
> he shall direct thy paths.
>
> **"**

Proverbs 3:5–6

And ye now therefore
have sorrow: but I will
see you again, and your
heart shall rejoice, and
your joy no man taketh
from you.

John 16:22

For I reckon that
the sufferings of this
present time are not
worthy to be compared
with the glory which
shall be revealed in us.

Romans 8:18

66

Blessed are ye that
hunger now: for ye
shall be filled. Blessed
are ye that weep now:
for ye shall laugh.

99

Luke 6:21

And seeing the multitudes,
he went up into a mountain:
and when he was set, his
disciples came unto him: And
he opened his mouth, and
taught them, saying, Blessed
are the poor in spirit: for theirs
is the kingdom of heaven.

Matthew 5:1–3

> **Let not your heart be troubled: ye believe in God, believe also in me.**

John 14:1

Be careful for nothing; but
in every thing by prayer
and supplication with
thanksgiving let your
requests be made known
unto God. And the peace
of God, which passeth all
understanding, shall keep
your hearts and minds
through Christ Jesus.

Philippians 4:6–7

"

Finally, brethren whatsoever
things are true, whatsoever
things are honest, whatsoever
things are just, whatsoever
things are pure, whatsoever
things are lovely, whatsoever
things are of good report; if
there be any virtue, and if
there be any praise, think on
these things.

"

Philippians 4:8

Surely he hath borne
our griefs, and carried
our sorrows: yet
we did esteem him
stricken, smitten of
God, and afflicted.

Isaiah 53:4

> And we know that all things work together for good to them that love God, to them who are the called according to his purpose.

Romans 8:28

To every thing there is a
season, and a time to every
purpose under the heaven:
A time to be born, and a time to
die; a time to plant, and a time to
pluck up that which is planted;
A time to kill, and a time to heal;
a time to break down, and a time
to build up; A time to weep, and
a time to laugh; a time to mourn,
and a time to dance…

Ecclesiastes 3:1–4

66

But I would not have you to be
ignorant, brethren, concerning
them which are asleep, that
ye sorrow not, even as others
which have no hope. For if we
believe that Jesus died and
rose again, even so them also
which sleep in Jesus
will God bring with him.

99

1 Thessalonians 4:13–14

66

Blessed be God, even the
Father of our Lord Jesus Christ,
the Father of mercies, and the God
of all comfort; Who comforteth us
in all our tribulation, that we may
be able to comfort them which
are in any trouble, by the comfort
wherewith we ourselves are
comforted of God.

99

2 Corinthians 1:3–4

I have fought a good fight,
I have finished my course,
I have kept the faith:
Henceforth there is laid up for
me a crown of righteousness,
which the Lord, the righteous
judge, shall give me at that
day: and not to me only, but
unto all them also that love
his appearing.

2 Timothy 4:7–8

> Yea, though I walk through the valley of the shadow of death, I will fear no evil: for thou art with me; thy rod and thy staff they comfort me.

Psalm 23:4

For our light affliction, which is but for a moment, worketh for us a far more exceeding and eternal weight of glory; While we look not at the things which are seen, but at the things which are not seen: for the things which are seen are temporal; but the things which are not seen are eternal.

2 Corinthians 4:17–18

CHAPTER

3

WORDS OF WISDOM

*They say a wise man knows
he knows nothing – so let these
verses be your guide when the
path forward is unclear.*

The fear of the Lord
is the beginning of
knowledge: but fools
despise wisdom and
instruction.

Proverbs 1:7

66

Trust in the Lord
with all thine heart; and
lean not unto thine own
understanding. In all thy
ways acknowledge him,
and he shall direct
thy paths.

99

Proverbs 3:5–6

If any of you lack wisdom, let him ask of God, that giveth to all men liberally, and upbraideth not; and it shall be given him.

James 1:5

> Let no man deceive you with vain words: for because of these things cometh the wrath of God upon the children of disobedience. Be not ye therefore partakers with them. For ye were sometimes darkness, but now are ye light in the Lord: walk as children of light: (For the fruit of the Spirit is in all goodness and righteousness and truth;) Proving what is acceptable unto the Lord.

Ephesians 5:6–10

Beloved, believe not every spirit, but try the spirits whether they are of God: because many false prophets are gone out into the world.

1 John 4:1

66

And be not conformed
to this world: but be
ye transformed by the
renewing of your mind, that
ye may prove what is that
good, and acceptable, and
perfect, will of God.

99

Romans 12:2

Who is a wise man and endued
with knowledge among you?
let him shew out of a good
conversation his works with
meekness of wisdom. But if ye
have bitter envying and strife in
your hearts, glory not, and lie not
against the truth. This wisdom
descendeth not from above, but is
earthly, sensual, devilish…

…For where envying and strife is, there is confusion and every evil work. But the wisdom that is from above is first pure, then peaceable, gentle, and easy to be intreated, full of mercy and good fruits, without partiality, and without hypocrisy. And the fruit of righteousness is sown in peace of them that make peace.

James 3:13–18

Therefore whosoever
heareth these sayings of
mine, and doeth them,
I will liken him unto a
wise man, which built his
house upon a rock…

Matthew 7:24

66

And this I pray, that your love
may abound yet more and
more in knowledge and in all
judgment; That ye may approve
things that are excellent; that
ye may be sincere and without
offence till the day of Christ.

99

Philippians 1:9–10

"

O the depth of the riches both
of the wisdom and knowledge
of God! how unsearchable are
his judgments, and his ways past
finding out! For who hath known
the mind of the Lord? or who hath
been his counsellor? Or who hath
first given to him, and it shall be
recompensed unto him again?

"

Romans 11:33–35

66

But unto them which are called, both Jews and Greeks, Christ the power of God, and the wisdom of God.

99

1 Corinthians 1:24

[Wisdom] is more precious than rubies: and all the things thou canst desire are not to be compared unto her.

Proverbs 3:15

> 66
>
> The wise in
> heart will receive
> commandments:
> but a prating fool
> shall fall.
>
> 99

Proverbs 10:8

Get wisdom, get understanding: forget it not; neither decline from the words of my mouth. Forsake her not, and she shall preserve thee: love her, and she shall keep thee.

Proverbs 4:5–6

> Wisdom is the principal
> thing; therefore get wisdom:
> and with all thy getting get
> understanding. Exalt her, and
> she shall promote thee: she shall
> bring thee to honour, when
> thou dost embrace her.

Proverbs 4:7–8

"

For by me thy days
shall be multiplied, and
the years of thy life shall
be increased. If thou be
wise, thou shalt be wise
for thyself: but if thou
scornest, thou alone
shalt bear it.

"

Proverbs 9:11–12

66

And unto man he
said, Behold, the
fear of the Lord, that
is wisdom; and to
depart from evil is
understanding.

99

Job 28:28

81

So teach us to
number our days,
that we may apply
our hearts unto
wisdom.

Psalm 90:12

> **66**
>
> Happy is the
> man that findeth
> wisdom, and the
> man that getteth
> understanding.
>
> **99**

Proverbs 3:13

She openeth her
mouth with wisdom;
and in her tongue is
the law of kindness.

Proverbs 31:26

66

For wisdom is a
defence, and money
is a defence: but the
excellency of knowledge
is, that wisdom giveth
life to them that
have it.

99

Ecclesiastes 7:12

66

And God gave
Solomon wisdom and
understanding exceeding
much, and largeness
of heart, even as the
sand that is on the
sea shore.

99

1 Kings 4:29

66

For the Lord
giveth wisdom:
out of his
mouth cometh
knowledge and
understanding.

99

Proverbs 2:6

Let no man deceive himself. If any man among you seemeth to be wise in this world, let him become a fool, that he may be wise.

1 Corinthians 3:18

66

It is as sport to a
fool to do mischief:
but a man of
understanding
hath wisdom.

99

Proverbs 10:23

> **When pride cometh,
> then cometh shame:
> but with the lowly
> is wisdom.**

Proverbs 11:2

66

The way of a fool is right in his own eyes: but he that hearkeneth unto counsel is wise.

99

Proverbs 12:15

Every wise woman buildeth
her house: but the foolish
plucketh it down with her
hands. He that walketh in his
uprightness feareth the Lord:
but he that is perverse
in his ways despiseth him.

Proverbs 14:1–2

A scorner loveth not one
that reproveth him: neither
will he go unto the wise.
A merry heart maketh a
cheerful countenance: but
by sorrow of the heart the
spirit is broken.

Proverbs 15:12–13

> The fear of
> the Lord is the
> instruction
> of wisdom; and
> before honour
> is humility.

Proverbs 15:33

> ❝
>
> The heart of the
> prudent getteth
> knowledge; and the
> ear of the wise
> seeketh knowledge.
>
> ❞

Proverbs 18:15

66

Hear counsel,
and receive
instruction, that
thou mayest be
wise in thy
latter end.

99

Proverbs 19:20

66

Bow down thine ear, and
hear the words of the wise,
and apply thine heart unto
my knowledge. For it is a
pleasant thing if thou keep
them within thee; they shall
withal be fitted in thy lips.
That thy trust may be in the
Lord, I have made known
to thee this day, even to thee.

99

Proverbs 22:17–19

Through wisdom is
an house builded; and
by understanding it is
established: And by
knowledge shall the
chambers be filled
with all precious and
pleasant riches...

...A wise man is strong;
yea, a man of knowledge
increaseth strength. For
by wise counsel thou shalt
make thy war: and in
multitude of counsellors
there is safety. Wisdom
is too high for a fool: he
openeth not his mouth
in the gate.

Proverbs 24:3–7

CHAPTER

4

WORDS OF ENCOURAGEMENT

Sometimes all we need is a boost when motivation is lacking – in which case, these verses have got you covered.

> 66
> Wherefore comfort yourselves together, and edify one another, even as also ye do.
> 99

1 Thessalonians 5:11

> Therefore, my beloved brethren, be ye stedfast, unmoveable, always abounding in the work of the Lord, forasmuch as ye know that your labour is not in vain in the Lord.

1 Corinthians 15:58

> These things I have spoken unto you, that in me ye might have peace. In the world ye shall have tribulation: but be of good cheer; I have overcome the world.

John 16:33

> **"**
>
> Ye are the light of the world. A city that is set on an hill cannot be hid. Neither do men light a candle, and put it under a bushel, but on a candlestick; and it giveth light unto all that are in the house. Let your light so shine before men, that they may see your good works, and glorify your Father which is in heaven.
>
> **"**

Matthew 5:14–16

But Jesus beheld them, and said unto them, With men this is impossible; but with God all things are possible.

Matthew 19:26

Therefore I say unto you,
What things soever ye
desire, when ye pray, believe
that ye receive them, and ye
shall have them.

Mark 11:24

66

I will lift up mine
eyes unto the hills, from
whence cometh my help.
My help cometh from
the Lord, which made
heaven and earth.

99

Psalm 121:1–2

> **The Lord shall fight for you, and ye shall hold your peace.**

Exodus 14:14

But seek ye first the kingdom of God, and his righteousness; and all these things shall be added unto you.

Matthew 6:33

66

And let us consider one another
to provoke unto love and to
good works: Not forsaking
the assembling of ourselves
together, as the manner of some
is; but exhorting one another:
and so much the more, as ye
see the day approaching.

99

Hebrews 10:24–25

In all labour there is profit: but the talk of the lips tendeth only to penury.

Proverbs 14:23

And let the beauty
of the Lord our God be
upon us: and establish
thou the work of our
hands upon us; yea,
the work of our hands
establish thou it.

Psalm 90:17

For which cause
we faint not; but
though our outward
man perish, yet
the inward man is
renewed day by day.

2 Corinthians 4:16

And all this assembly
shall know that
the Lord saveth not
with sword and
spear: for the battle
is the Lord's, and
he will give you into
our hands.

1 Samuel 17:47

Blessed are ye, when men
shall revile you, and persecute
you, and shall say all manner
of evil against you falsely,
for my sake. Rejoice, and be
exceeding glad: for great is
your reward in heaven: for so
persecuted they the prophets
which were before you.

Matthew 5:11–12

I am the vine, ye are the branches: He that abideth in me, and I in him, the same bringeth forth much fruit: for without me ye can do nothing. If a man abide not in me, he is cast forth as a branch, and is withered; and men gather them, and cast them into the fire, and they are burned. If ye abide in me, and my words abide in you, ye shall ask what ye will, and it shall be done unto you.

John 15:5–7

Behold, God is my
salvation; I will trust, and
not be afraid: for the Lord
Jehovah is my strength and
my song; he also is become
my salvation.

Isaiah 12:2

> ❝
>
> Trust in the Lord,
> and do good; so shalt
> thou dwell in the land,
> and verily thou
> shalt be fed.
>
> ❞

Psalm 37:3

The steps of a good man
are ordered by the Lord:
and he delighteth in his
way. Though he fall, he shall
not be utterly cast down:
for the Lord upholdeth him
with his hand.

Psalm 37:23–24

Jesus said unto her, I am
the resurrection, and the life:
he that believeth in me, though
he were dead, yet shall he live:
And whosoever liveth and
believeth in me shall never die.
Believest thou this?

John 11:25–26

For the Lord will not cast off for ever: But though he cause grief, yet will he have compassion according to the multitude of his mercies.

Lamentations 3:31–32

66

And let us not be weary in well doing: for in due season we shall reap, if we faint not.

99

Galatians 6:9

I can do all
things through
Christ which
strengtheneth me.

Philippians 4:13

When thou passest through the waters, I will be with thee; and through the rivers, they shall not overflow thee: when thou walkest through the fire, thou shalt not be burned; neither shall the flame kindle upon thee.

Isaiah 43:2

And whatsoever
ye do, do it heartily,
as to the Lord, and
not unto men.

Colossians 3:23

Now faith is the substance of things hoped for, the evidence of things not seen.

Hebrews 11:1

CHAPTER

5

WORDS OF JOY

Life isn't all doom and gloom, as hard as it is to see sometimes – so remember to celebrate it when you can!

And the children of Israel
that were present at Jerusalem
kept the feast of unleavened
bread seven days with great
gladness: and the Levites and
the priests praised the Lord
day by day, singing with loud
instruments unto the Lord.

2 Chronicles 30:21

It is of the Lord's mercies that we are not consumed, because his compassions fail not. They are new every morning: great is thy faithfulness. The Lord is my portion, saith my soul; therefore will I hope in him. The Lord is good unto them that wait for him, to the soul that seeketh him. It is good that a man should both hope and quietly wait for the salvation of the Lord.

Lamentations 3:22–26

Thou wilt shew me
the path of life: in thy
presence is fulness of
joy; at thy right hand
there are pleasures
for evermore.

Psalm 16:11

It is a good thing to give
thanks unto the Lord, and to
sing praises unto thy name,
O Most High: To shew forth
thy lovingkindness in the
morning, and thy faithfulness
every night…

Psalm 92:1–2

Fear not, O land;
be glad and rejoice:
for the Lord will do
great things.

Joel 2:21

And bring hither the
fatted calf, and kill it; and
let us eat, and be merry:
For this my son was dead,
and is alive again; he was
lost, and is found. And they
began to be merry.

Luke 15:23–24

He hath made every thing beautiful in his time: also he hath set the world in their heart, so that no man can find out the work that God maketh from the beginning to the end. I know that there is no good in them, but for a man to rejoice, and to do good in his life…

…And also that every man
should eat and drink, and enjoy
the good of all his labour, it is
the gift of God.

Ecclesiastes 3:11–13

66

This is the day which
the Lord hath made;
we will rejoice and be
glad in it.

99

Psalm 118:24

66

What will ye do in
the solemn day, and
in the day of the feast
of the Lord?

99

Hosea 9:5

Therefore let us keep the feast, not with old leaven, neither with the leaven of malice and wickedness; but with the unleavened bread of sincerity and truth.

1 Corinthians 5:8

Rejoice in the Lord always: and again I say, Rejoice.

Philippians 4:4

I will mention the loving
kindnesses of the Lord, and the
praises of the Lord, according to
all that the Lord hath bestowed
on us, and the great goodness
toward the house of Israel, which
he hath bestowed on them
according to his mercies, and
according to the multitude of
his loving kindnesses.

Isaiah 63:7

Surely goodness and mercy shall follow me all the days of my life: and I will dwell in the house of the Lord for ever.

Psalm 23:6

The heart of him that
hath understanding
seeketh knowledge: but the
mouth of fools feedeth on
foolishness. All the days of
the afflicted are evil: but he
that is of a merry heart hath
a continual feast.

Proverbs 15:14–15

"

And Hezekiah spake
comfortably unto all the
Levites that taught the good
knowledge of the Lord: and
they did eat throughout the
feast seven days, offering
peace offerings, and making
confession to the Lord God
of their fathers.

"

2 Chronicles 30:22

> **For by me thy days shall be multiplied, and the years of thy life shall be increased.**

Proverbs 9:11

And when he had brought
them into his house, he
set meat before them, and
rejoiced, believing in God
with all his house.

Acts 16:34

Rejoice greatly,
O daughter of Zion; shout,
O daughter of Jerusalem:
behold, thy King cometh
unto thee: he is just, and
having salvation; lowly, and
riding upon an ass, and upon
a colt the foal of an ass.

Zechariah 9:9

"

When I remember these things,
I pour out my soul in me: for
I had gone with the multitude,
I went with them to the house
of God, with the voice of joy
and praise, with a multitude
that kept holyday.

"

Psalm 42:4

And whether one member suffer, all the members suffer with it; or one member be honoured, all the members rejoice with it.

1 Corinthians 12:26

> The Lord thy God in the midst of thee is mighty; he will save, he will rejoice over thee with joy; he will rest in his love, he will joy over thee with singing.

Zephaniah 3:17

And thou shalt bestow that
money for whatsoever thy
soul lusteth after, for oxen,
or for sheep, or for wine,
or for strong drink, or for
whatsoever thy soul desireth:
and thou shalt eat there
before the Lord thy God, and
thou shalt rejoice, thou, and
thine household...

Deuteronomy 14:26

66

Whom having not
seen, ye love; in whom,
though now ye see
him not, yet believing,
ye rejoice with joy
unspeakable and full
of glory…

99

1 Peter 1:8

Let the saints be joyful in glory: let them sing aloud upon their beds.

Psalm 149:5

66

Pray without ceasing.
In every thing give
thanks: for this is the will
of God in Christ Jesus
concerning you. Quench
not the Spirit.

99

1 Thessalonians 5:17–19

These things have I spoken unto you, that my joy might remain in you, and that your joy might be full.

John 15:11

But rejoice, in a smuch
as ye are partakers
of Christ's sufferings;
that, when his glory
shall be revealed, ye
may be glad also with
exceeding joy.

1 Peter 4:13

Praise ye the Lord. Praise
God in his sanctuary: praise
him in the firmament of his
power. Praise him for his mighty
acts: praise him according to his
excellent greatness. Praise him
with the sound of the trumpet:
praise him with the psaltery
and harp…

...Praise him with the timbrel and dance: praise him with stringed instruments and organs. Praise him upon the loud cymbals: praise him upon the high sounding cymbals. Let every thing that hath breath praise the Lord. Praise ye the Lord.

Psalm 150:1–6

Glory ye in his holy name: let the heart of them rejoice that seek the Lord.

1 Chronicles 16:10

And he said unto him,
Son, thou art ever with me,
and all that I have is thine.
It was meet that we should
make merry, and be glad:
for this thy brother was
dead, and is alive again;
and was lost, and is found.

Luke 15:31–32

CHAPTER

6

WORDS OF HOPE

When you feel lost and helpless, let these words of hope be a light at the end of the tunnel.

Now the God of
hope fill you with
all joy and peace in
believing, that ye
may abound in hope,
through the power of
the Holy Ghost.

Romans 15:13

But they that wait upon the Lord shall renew their strength; they shall mount up with wings as eagles; they shall run, and not be weary; and they shall walk, and not faint.

Isaiah 40:31

And not only so, but we glory
in tribulations also: knowing
that tribulation worketh patience;
And patience, experience; and
experience, hope: And hope
maketh not ashamed; because
the love of God is shed abroad
in our hearts by the Holy Ghost
which is given unto us.

Romans 5:3–5

Fear thou not; for I am
with thee: be not dismayed;
for I am thy God: I will
strengthen thee; yea, I will
help thee; yea, I will uphold
thee with the right hand of
my righteousness.

Isaiah 41:10

For I know the
thoughts that I think
toward you, saith
the Lord, thoughts
of peace, and not of
evil, to give you an
expected end.

Jeremiah 29:11

It is of the Lord's
mercies that we are not
consumed, because
his compassions fail
not. They are new every
morning: great is thy
faithfulness.

Lamentations 3:22–23

Be ye strong therefore, and let not your hands be weak: for your work shall be rewarded.

2 Chronicles 15:7

A new heart also will I
give you, and a new spirit
will I put within you: and
I will take away the stony
heart out of your flesh,
and I will give you an
heart of flesh.

Ezekiel 36:26

66

And rend your heart, and
not your garments, and turn
unto the Lord your God: for
he is gracious and merciful,
slow to anger, and of great
kindness, and repenteth
him of the evil.

99

Joel 2:13

Then spake Jesus
again unto them, saying,
I am the light of the
world: he that followeth
me shall not walk in
darkness, but shall have
the light of life.

John 8:12

Nay, in all these things we are
more than conquerors through
him that loved us. For I am
persuaded, that neither death, nor
life, nor angels, nor principalities,
nor powers, nor things present,
nor things to come, Nor height,
nor depth, nor any other creature,
shall be able to separate us from
the love of God, which is in
Christ Jesus our Lord.

Romans 8:37–39

66

And, behold,
I come quickly; and
my reward is with
me, to give every
man according as
his work shall be.

99

Revelation 22:12

66

For whatsoever
things were written
aforetime were written
for our learning, that we
through patience and
comfort of the scriptures
might have hope.

99

Romans 15:4

"

Rejoicing in
hope; patient
in tribulation;
continuing instant
in prayer…

"

Romans 12:12

Now faith is the substance of things hoped for, the evidence of things not seen.

Hebrews 11:1

For we are saved by
hope: but hope that is seen
is not hope: for what a man
seeth, why doth he yet hope
for? But if we hope for that
we see not, then do we with
patience wait for it.

Romans 8:24–25

Therefore I will
look unto the Lord;
I will wait for the
God of my salvation:
my God will hear me.

Micah 7:7

In hope of eternal
life, which God,
that cannot lie,
promised before
the world began.

Titus 1:2

Through faith also Sara herself received strength to conceive seed, and was delivered of a child when she was past age, because she judged him faithful who had promised.

Hebrews 11:11

Let us hold fast
the profession of
our faith without
wavering; (for he
is faithful that
promised)...

Hebrews 10:23

> **Let thy mercy, O Lord, be upon us, according as we hope in thee.**

Psalm 33:22

> **But I will hope
> continually, and
> will yet praise thee
> more and more.**

Psalm 71:14

I wait for
the Lord, my
soul doth wait,
and in his word
do I hope.

Psalm 130:5

For the needy
shall not always
be forgotten: the
expectation of the
poor shall not
perish for ever.

Psalm 9:18

"

Many there be which say
of my soul, There is no help
for him in God. Selah. But
thou, O Lord, art a shield for
me; my glory, and the lifter
up of mine head. I cried unto
the Lord with my voice, and
he heard me out of his
holy hill. Selah…

…I laid me down and
slept; I awaked; for
the Lord sustained me.
I will not be afraid of ten
thousands of people, that
have set themselves against
me round about.

Psalm 3:2–6

The eyes of your
understanding being
enlightened; that ye may
know what is the hope
of his calling, and what
the riches of the glory of
his inheritance in
the saints…

Ephesians 1:18

" Who delivered us
from so great a death,
and doth deliver: in
whom we trust that he
will yet deliver us. "

2 Corinthians 1:10

Jesus said unto him,
If thou canst believe, all
things are possible to
him that believeth.

Mark 9:23